A Torch FOR FREEDOM

BUILDING THE STATUE OF LIBERTY

Virginia Loh-Hagan

45TH PARALLEL PRESS

Published in the United States of America by Cherry Lake Publishing
Ann Arbor, Michigan
www.cherrylakepublishing.com

Reading Adviser: Beth Walker Gambro, MS, Ed., Reading Consultant, Yorkville, IL
Cover Designer: Felicia Macheske

Photo Credits: © jaquelinetdc/Shutterstock.com, cover, 1; © Courtesy of the Library of Congress, LC-USZ62-18087, 5; © Everett Historical/Shutterstock.com, 6; © Courtesy of the Library of Congress, LC-USZ62-18086, 11; © Courtesy of the Library of Congress, LC-USZ62-20115, 12; © JohnatAPW/Shutterstock.com, 17; © Courtesy of the Library of Congress, LC-USZ62-20113, 19; © rarrarorro/Shutterstock.com, 21; © Courtesy of the Library of Congress, LC-DIG-ppmsca-70733, 22; © Luciano Mortula/Shutterstock.com, 25

Graphic Elements Throughout: © Chipmunk131/Shutterstock.com; © Nowik Sylwia/Shutterstock.com; © Andrey_Popov/Shutterstock.com; © NadzeyaShanchuk/Shutterstock.com; © KathyGold/Shutterstock.com; © Black creator/Shutterstock.com; © Edvard Molnar/Shutterstock.com; © Elenadesign/Shutterstock.com; © estherpoon/Shutterstock.com

45th Parallel Press is an imprint of Cherry Lake Publishing.

Library of Congress Cataloging-in-Publication Data
Names: Loh-Hagan, Virginia, author.
Title: A torch for freedom : building the Statue of Liberty / by Virginia Loh-Hagan.
Other titles: Building the Statue of Liberty
Description: Ann Arbor, Michigan : Cherry Lake Publishing, [2022] | Series: Behind the curtain | Includes index.
Identifiers: LCCN 2021037488 | ISBN 9781534199514 (hardcover) | ISBN 9781668900659 (paperback) |
    ISBN 9781668906415 (ebook) | ISBN 9781668902097 (pdf)
Subjects: LCSH: Statue of Liberty (New York, N.Y.)—Juvenile literature.
Classification: LCC F128.64.L6 L64 2022 | DDC 974.7/1—dc23
LC record available at https://lccn.loc.gov/2021037488

Cherry Lake Publishing would like to acknowledge the work of the Partnership for 21st Century Learning, a Network of Battelle for Kids. Please visit *http://www.battelleforkids.org/networks/p21* for more information.

Printed in the United States of America
Corporate Graphics

A Note on Dramatic Retellings

Participating in Readers Theater, or dramatic retellings, can greatly improve reading skills, especially fluency. The books in the **BEHIND THE CURTAIN** series give readers opportunities to learn about important historical events in a fun and engaging way. These books serve as a bridge to more complex texts. All the characters and stories have been fictionalized. To learn more, check out the Perspectives Library series and the Modern Perspectives series, as **BEHIND THE CURTAIN** books are aligned to these stories.

TABLE of CONTENTS

HISTORICAL BACKGROUND

The Statue of Liberty stands for freedom and democracy. It was a gift. The people of France gave it to the United States. The statue honors the friendship between the 2 nations. It was completed in 1886.

It's 305 feet (93 meters) tall. It's made of copper. The statue is a figure of Libertas, the Roman goddess of liberty. She is wearing a robe. Her right hand is raised. It holds a torch. Her left hand holds a tablet. The date "July 4, 1776" is written on the tablet. This date is when the Declaration of Independence was finalized. Broken chains lie at her feet. This represents the abolition of slavery. It also represents freedom from harsh rule.

FLASH FACT!

Today, more than 10 million Americans say they have a French background.

Vocabulary

tablet (TA-bluht) a flat slab of stone, clay, or wood with words written on it

abolition (ah-buh-LIH-shuhn) ending or stopping something

slavery (SLAY-vuh-ree) a system of owning and enslaving people

FLASH FACT!

More than 1 million immigrants arrive in the United States each year.

Vocabulary

pedestal (PEH-duh-stuhl)
the base on which a statue is mounted

assembled (uh-SEM-buhld) put together separate pieces to create a whole

immigration center
(ih-muh-GRAY-shuhn SEN-tuhr)
a place that processes people who want to settle in a new country

Frédéric Auguste Bartholdi was a French sculptor. He designed the statue. Gustave Eiffel was a French engineer. He designed the metal framework. The statue was built in France. It was shipped to the United States in pieces. American builders made the pedestal and assembled the statue.

The statue is on a small island in Upper New York Bay. Every ship entering New York Harbor can see it. This area became known as the "gateway to America." It's close to Ellis Island. Ellis Island was an immigration center. More than 12 million immigrants were processed there. The statue became a welcoming symbol to immigrants.

CAST of CHARACTERS

NARRATOR: person who helps tells the story

ARMAND: a French **laborer** in the 1880s

SAMMY: an American laborer in the 1880s

ASHLEY: an American news reporter in the 1880s

MIKE: a young White male student in 2022

KATHLEEN: a young female Irish American student in 2022

TAM: a young female Vietnamese American student in 2022 whose family are **refugees**

SPOTLIGHT
AMPLIFICATION OF AN ACTIVIST

Sophie Cruz became an immigrant rights activist at 5 years old. The pope is the head of the Roman Catholic Church. In 2015, Pope Francis visited Washington, D.C. She handed him a letter. She wrote, "I want to tell you that my heart is sad. And I would like to ask you to speak with the president and the congress in legalizing my parents because every day I am scared they will be taken away from me." Cruz was born in the United States. Her parents emigrated from Oaxaca, Mexico. They're undocumented. This means they don't have the legal paperwork to be in the country. They could be sent back to Mexico. Cruz fights to continue DAPA. DAPA is Deferred Action for Parents of Americans and Lawful Permanent Residents. This program would allow her parents to stay in the United States legally.

Vocabulary
laborer (LAY-buhr-uhr) worker

refugees (REH-fyoo-jeez) people who have been forced to leave their country in order to escape war, persecution, or natural disasters

FLASH FACT!
Since 1975, the United States has welcomed more than 3 million refugees from all over the world.

ACT 1

NARRATOR: *On October 28, 1886, there was a party to celebrate the Statue of Liberty.* **ARMAND** *and* **SAMMY** *had helped build the statue. They're in the crowd.*

ARMAND: There must be a million people here!

SAMMY: This is a big deal for us New Yorkers.

ARMAND: This is a big deal for me too. I've been waiting 10 years for this.

SAMMY: Why 10 years? That's a long time.

ARMAND: I am from France. I worked on the statue. I helped build it.

SAMMY: I'm excited to see Lady Liberty.

ARMAND: Lady Liberty? The French people call her the Lady of the Park.

SAMMY: Why is that?

FLASH FACT!

The official name of the statue is "Liberty Enlightening the World."

ARMAND: There weren't any indoor spaces big enough to fit the statue. We had to work in a park. It was fun. People walked by. They liked seeing work progress on the "Lady of the Park."

SAMMY: I also had to work outdoors.

ARMAND: Did you help build the statue as well?

SAMMY: Yes, I worked on the pedestal. I worked from dawn to dusk. I spent hours digging. I had to dig out a big area. I also helped build the base using bricks and **mortar**.

ARMAND: You need a strong **foundation** to support our Lady. She is huge.

SAMMY: I knew she was going to be big. But I didn't realize how big. The pedestal had to be strong enough to support a lot of weight. It also had to withstand the salty ocean air and strong winds.

Vocabulary

mortar (MOHR-tuhr) a mixture used for building that hardens

foundation (fown-DAY-shuhn) a strong structure that supports buildings from under the ground

FLASH FACT!

The statue arrived in 350 pieces.

ARMAND: It must have been difficult.

SAMMY: It was hard and messy. What was the work like for you?

ARMAND: Same. I was always covered in dust. I had to focus really hard. I also had to use **precise** measurements. We couldn't be off by even a little bit. If we were, the entire thing would have to be rebuilt.

SAMMY: I can't believe the statue is finally done. I'm so proud of what we've done.

ARMAND: It's great how our countries worked together.

SAMMY: It was worth all the aches and pains.

ARMAND: I agree. For me, the statue represents France's strong support for the United States.

SPOTLIGHT
A SPECIAL EFFECT

The Statue of Liberty has been in many movies. It has been destroyed in several of them. Its destruction symbolizes the end of humanity. This makes for good drama. But it's true that the Statue of Liberty isn't unbreakable. The statue is strong and can survive heavy winds. It would be hard to destroy or move. But it is no match for climate change. Climate change is a long-term change in weather patterns. Human activities are negatively affecting the planet. The world is getting hotter. Sea levels are rising. Ocean storms are increasing and are more violent. The Statue of Liberty could be destroyed by rising tides and water damage. For example, Hurricane Sandy happened in 2012. It flooded the statue's island. It caused more than $77 million in damages. Treat our planet better. Save the statue!

Vocabulary
precise (prih-SYS) exact

FLASH FACT!

Women were banned from attending the ceremony on the island. Women activists got a boat. They held their own party in the harbor.

SAMMY: For me, it represents freedom. I'm an immigrant. I was grateful for this work. Building the pedestal gave jobs and money to hundreds of immigrants.

NARRATOR: *Sammy is still at the party.* **ASHLEY**, *a reporter, arrives.*

SAMMY: Why are people throwing paper out the windows?

ASHLEY: That's **ticker tape**. The parade is going by the New York Stock Exchange. There are **traders** there. They use ticker tape as part of their job.

SAMMY: It looks like snow. What fun! We should do this at all parades!

ASHLEY: I want to interview you for an article. I want to know what you think about the statue.

SAMMY: This statue means a lot to me. I helped build it. I also helped pay for it.

ASHLEY: That's amazing. I work for Joseph Pulitzer. He started the **fundraising campaign**. He owns *The New York World* newspaper.

SAMMY: That's where I read about it. Remind me why you needed to raise money?

ASHLEY: The French paid for the statue. But we had to pay for the pedestal. We ran out of money.

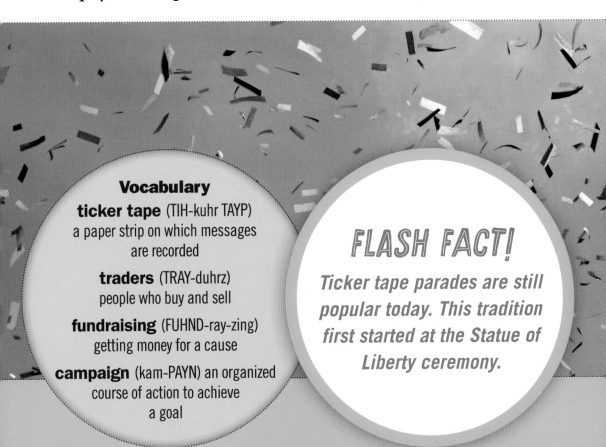

Vocabulary

ticker tape (TIH-kuhr TAYP) a paper strip on which messages are recorded

traders (TRAY-duhrz) people who buy and sell

fundraising (FUHND-ray-zing) getting money for a cause

campaign (kam-PAYN) an organized course of action to achieve a goal

FLASH FACT!
Ticker tape parades are still popular today. This tradition first started at the Statue of Liberty ceremony.

SAMMY: I remember having to stop working. The pedestal was only half complete.

ASHLEY: It would have been such a disgrace if we couldn't finish the pedestal. We printed an article about needing money. Thanks to you and many others, we raised enough.

SAMMY: I didn't have much money to spare. But I sent what I had.

ASHLEY: That's exactly what we needed. Many working-class people sent in what they could.

SAMMY: I sent in only a few cents. But I still got my name published in the paper. That's something!

ASHLEY: It was amazing. We had more than 125,000 **donors** from all over the country. We raised more than $100,000.

SAMMY: It was an honor to be a part of this. Immigrants and workers like me helped build the Statue of Liberty.

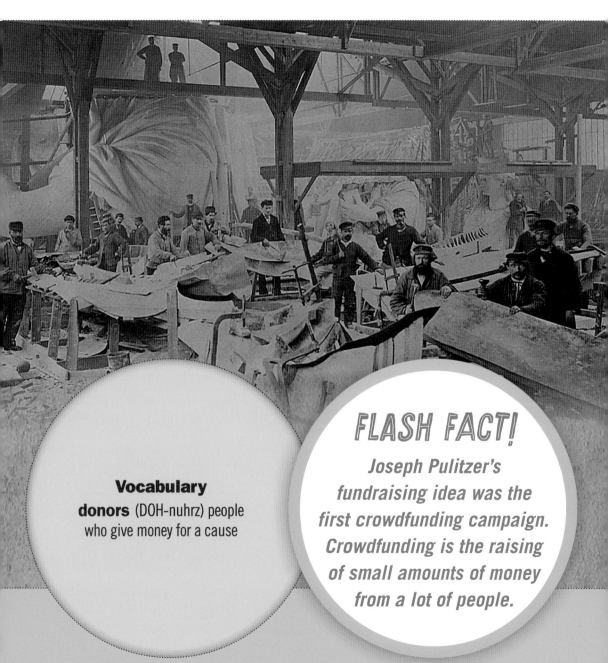

Vocabulary
donors (DOH-nuhrz) people who give money for a cause

FLASH FACT!
Joseph Pulitzer's fundraising idea was the first crowdfunding campaign. Crowdfunding is the raising of small amounts of money from a lot of people.

ACT 2

NARRATOR: *It is the year 2022.* **MIKE, KATHLEEN,** *and* **TAM** *are students. They're from a local school. They're on a school field trip. They're touring the Statue of Liberty.*

MIKE: Want to hear a fun fact? The statue arrived in pieces. The torch was the first part of the statue to get here.

KATHLEEN: My family came through Ellis Island. They wrote that the torch was lighting their way to freedom.

MIKE: Where did your family come from?

KATHLEEN: They escaped from Ireland.

TAM: Why did they have to flee?

KATHLEEN: Things were bad. They came to the United States for a better life.

FLASH FACT!

Since 1916, people can't go up into the torch. Today, people can access the TorchCam. This is a camera at the torch. It allows people to see the views from the torch balcony.

TAM: My family came here for a better life too. During the 1970s, there was a war in Vietnam. My family had to escape the war. They came to the United States as refugees.

Vocabulary

colossus (kuh-LAH-suhss) a statue that is much bigger than life size

huddled (HUH-duhld) crowded together

masses (MA-suhz) large groups of people

yearning (YUHR-ning) wanting or needing

FLASH FACT!

Many Vietnamese people fled Vietnam by sea. They became known as "boat people."

MIKE: Did they see the torch like Kathleen's family?

TAM: No. My family came on a plane. They landed at Camp Pendleton. That's in San Diego, California. Then my grandparents moved to New York.

KATHLEEN: Have they seen the Statue of Liberty yet?

TAM: Of course. It was one of the first places they visited. When I was old enough to read, they made me read Emma Lazarus' poem.

MIKE: There's a poem?

TAM: The title is "The New **Colossus**." It's on the pedestal. It's right here.

MIKE: "Give me your tired, your poor, your **huddled masses yearning** to breathe free...."

KATHLEEN: Why did your grandparents like that poem so much?

TAM: They respect Lazarus. She was an American Jewish **activist**. She learned about the Russian **pogroms**. Many Jewish people were killed. Lazarus had to do something. She helped many Jewish refugees immigrate here. She set up a school to train them for jobs.

MIKE: What does that have to do with the poem?

TAM: Lazarus was also a poet. At first, she said no to writing this poem. She didn't want to write about a statue. But she wanted to express her **empathy** for the Jewish refugees. She did this with her poem.

KATHLEEN: The poem reminds us that we're a nation of immigrants. It reminds us of our duty to care for others.

MIKE: My parents have said some mean things about immigrants.

Vocabulary

activist (AK-tih-vist) a person who fights for political or social change

pogroms (POH-gruhmz) organized massacres of people or ethnic groups

empathy (EM-puh-thee) the ability to understand and share the feelings of another

FLASH FACT!

In the 1940s, the United States turned away thousands of Jewish refugees. They feared they were Nazi spies.

TAM: Life is hard for immigrants. On the one hand, the Statue of Liberty welcomes immigrants. On the other hand, the United States often treats immigrants like **scapegoats**. They get blamed for all kinds of things.

KATHLEEN: In history, Irish Americans were **discriminated** against. We were blamed for taking away jobs. We were blamed for causing sicknesses. Many Irish Americans were beaten. Some were even killed.

TAM: Asian immigrants have faced the same thing. There are many examples of anti-Asian hate.

MIKE: Well, that happened a long time ago. Things are different now. They're much better.

TAM: Anti-Asian hate is still happening.

MIKE: What do you mean?

SPOTLIGHT

Patricia Okoumou is an immigrant from The Republic of Congo. She is a naturalized U.S. citizen. On July 4, 2018, she climbed the pedestal of the Statue of Liberty. This was illegal. She climbed to protest immigrant children being separated from their families at the border. She wanted to climb to the top. But the metal was slippery. She refused to come down. Police helicopters circled the statue. Okoumou stayed there for 8 hours before being arrested. On November 26, 2018, she illegally climbed the Eiffel Tower in Paris, France. She did this because the French gave the Statue of Liberty to the United States. She said, "I must continue." She wanted Americans to think about migrant children. Migrant children were taken from their parents. They were put in cages in detention camps. She said, "I was having nightmares about the children in cages."

Vocabulary

scapegoats (SKAYP-gohts) people blamed for wrongdoings, mistakes, or faults of others

discriminated (dih-SKRIH-muh-nay-tuhd) treated people unjustly or unfairly

FLASH FACT!

In 2020, anti-Asian hate crimes increased by 150 percent. Most crimes took place in New York and California.

TAM: Do you remember when people were calling COVID-19 "Kung Flu" or "China **Virus**?"

MIKE: Yes. That happened in 2020 at the start of the pandemic.

TAM: People blamed COVID-19 on people who look like me. Asian Americans were **harassed**. There was so much hate against us.

KATHLEEN: That's awful.

TAM: My father was walking to work. Someone called him names. They spit on him. We didn't feel safe. I was scared to leave my house.

KATHLEEN: I'm sorry that happened to you and your family.

MIKE: That is so wrong.

TAM: Immigrants are treated like the enemy. Asian Americans are still seen as **foreigners**. I was born here. My parents are **naturalized** citizens. But people still tell us to "go back home."

MIKE: Your home is here. People need to be better.

KATHLEEN: We have come a long way. But we still have a lot of work to do.

TAM: It's up to us to carry the torch of liberty.

Vocabulary

virus (VYE-ruhss) a type of germ that can make people sick

harassed (huh-RASST) bothered or disturbed someone

foreigners (FOHR-uh-nuhrz) people who are not from the United States

naturalized (NA-chuh-ruh-lyzd) went through the process of gaining legal citizenship

FLASH FACT!

After the 9/11 attacks, Americans who looked Middle Eastern were harassed.

FLASH FORWARD
CURRENT CONNECTIONS

The Statue of Liberty was built in 1886. But its legacy lives on. It still affects us. There is much work for us to do.

- **Stand against White supremacy:** The United States has a history of mistreating people of color. The statue celebrates the end of slavery. But Black Americans are still not free from injustice. To be true, we must fight for liberty for all. We must truly aim to live up to the statue's ideals. It's important to fight against anti-Blackness.

- **Fight against family separation:** In 2018, the United States started prosecuting undocumented immigrants in the criminal justice system. Families were separated. Adults were held in jails. Many were sent back to their countries. The children were sent to detention centers. They lived in poor conditions. The policy of family separations was later ended. But the damage was done. Many children have still not been reunited with their parents. It is important to treat all people like humans.

- **Don't be xenophobic:** Xenophobia is the dislike of people from different countries. It is discrimination against foreigners. It also means treating non-White people like outsiders. In the United States, we have called foreigners "aliens." This is insulting. President Joe Biden wants to reform immigration. He wants to remove "alien" from U.S. immigration laws. He wants to replace it with "noncitizen." Words matter. It is important to use respectful words.

CONSIDER THIS!

TAKE A POSITION! Frederick Douglass was an African American activist. He believed in free migration. This means people should be able to live in any country they choose. He said it was a human right that belonged to "no particular race, but belongs alike to all and to all alike." Do you agree with free migration or not? Argue your point with reasons and evidence.

SAY WHAT? Learn more about the history of Asian American immigration. Learn more about the history of Hispanic American immigration. Explain how immigrants of color are treated in the United States.

THINK ABOUT IT! Refugees need a home. They have escaped from terrible situations. What are the pros and cons of taking in refugees? Should the United States take in more refugees?

Learn More

Howard, Martin. *A World Full of Journeys: Over 50 Stories of Human Migration That Changed Our World.* London, UK: Frances Lincoln Children's Books, 2022.

Krull, Kathleen. *American Immigration: Our History, Our Stories.* New York, NY: Quill Tree Books, 2021.

Martin, Claudia. *Our World in Crisis: Immigration.* London, UK: Franklin Watts, 2021.

Qaiser, Annie. *The Story of the Statue of Liberty.* Ann Arbor, MI: Cherry Lake Publishing, 2014.

INDEX

ABOUT THE AUTHOR

Dr. Virginia Loh-Hagan is an author, former K-8 teacher, curriculum designer, and university professor. She's currently the director of the Asian Pacific Islander Desi American (APIDA) Center at San Diego State University. Her parents were immigrants. She lives in San Diego with her one very tall husband and two very naughty dogs.